TimeRight

TimeRight:

Take Realistic Control of Your 1440 Minutes
for Maximum Effectiveness and Sanity

Kevin Stacey, MBA
TrainRight Media

Train**Right**, Inc.
Training the *right* way

Ordering Information/Quantity sales:
Special discounts are available on quantity purchases by corpora-
tions, associations, and others. For details, contact the publisher at
the address below.
First Edition (v.1.2)
Published by TrainRight Media
ISBN-13: 978-0-692-87727-2
ISBN-10: 0692877274

TrainRight Media Division of TrainRight, Inc.
10 Valleywood Road Hopkinton, MA 01758 USA
1-800-603-7168 • 617-687-1295 (fax)

www.trainrightinc.com
info@trainrightinc.com

Table of Contents

Preface

The World Health Organization has called the US one of the least happy and most anxious of all developed countries. We have around 5% of the world's population but consume over half of the world's prescription drugs. A big reason for this is our go-go culture and invasive preoccupation with the things we think we need to get done, which gets in the way of having satisfying human connections. Technology has not helped the harried pace of our society or provided us with more peace of mind. Many of us live with a constant sense of guilt that we didn't accomplish enough, no matter how unrealistic our expectations were in the first place. But do you realize that if you did everything that needed to be done in your life in one day, you wouldn't be a human being? You'd be a superhero? Now more than ever people are hungry for time management solutions.

Everyone has a different spin on time management, what it means, and what its goals ought to be.

Here's what I think the goals ought to be and the purpose of this book, which is three-fold:

1.   To help you to feel better about your days. To be more satisfied and realistic with what you get done and accomplish, instead of feeling guilty and "shoulding" yourself about what you didn't get done. Far too many of us are going to bed disappointed, and it's hard to get enough rejuvenating sleep with those kinds of thoughts bouncing around in your head.

2.   To help you feel more in control of what's happening instead of feeling out of control with external forces pulling the strings. Mental health professionals tell us that the degree of control we feel we have in our lives is directly proportional to our mental well-being.

3.   To assist you in managing how others within your organization perceive you. Life is easier when you're viewed as somebody who is a high achiever and focuses on the most important organizational priorities. Often there is a disconnect between the perception and reality. Some people are too hard on themselves and some just think they're wonderful and have no concept of how they waste time or how they're perceived by others.

Introduction

Welcome to Time Right: take realistic control of your 1440 minutes for maximum effectiveness and sanity. I'm so glad you're investing the time to read it. Nowadays, more than ever, it seems that just about everybody is interested in time management and people are looking for solutions.

There are so many potential demands on our time, and there are so many people who would just love to waste your time and make their priorities your priorities. There is so much noise, distractions, and competing interests vying for your attention. For over twenty years, I've been fascinated with the concept of time management, and after teaching seminars on it for over seventeen years, I've come to realize that how we manage our time affects every aspect of our lives.

How well you feel you manage your time, and to a lesser extent, how the people around you feel about it, has a direct correlation to how satisfied you are with your life. It also has a tremendous effect on our health and is a root cause of much of our stress. The health manifestations of real or perceived poor time management are shocking. In addition to all the other major health problems, in the U.S. we have the highest percent of people wearing mouth guards and grinding their teeth of any industrialized society.

It's not like this in many other European nations wherein it seems that enjoying the moments of life is more valued than what you can produce in each moment. Americans, even though we have smaller allocations than most any other nation, don't take our allotted vacation time, and when we do, we rarely feel truly disconnected from work.

Companies are interested in time management because they want their people spending more time on higher value activities and less on lower. I can't blame employers for wanting to get as much productivity out of their people as possible. However, many organizations must acknowledge that time management can't compensate for a lack of resources. If ten people are needed in a department to meet the organization's goals for that department, but there are only six people, then those goals aren't going to be met. It doesn't mean those six people are failures or don't manage their time well.

Some people don't realize that the even the phrase "time management" is an oxymoron. Because you can't do it; you can't manage time. Time just does its thing; it just ticks away. It doesn't matter what we think or what we feel. We can't make it move any slower or faster. So, what should it be called? It should be called self-management as it relates to the passage of time. But that's not a catchy enough title that's easy for people to grasp.

Since it's not really about managing time, time management is most definitely about you. It's about the choices you make. It's about the things that you do and how long you spend on each item. It's about the order of things that you take on, what you choose to do first and because of that choice what is waiting on your back burner. It's also about the story you tell yourself about how you think you are doing with managing your time. It's about how realistic you are with yourself and others. It's about how controlling or not controlling you are. It's about what you say and how you say it. It's about the boundaries you set or don't set with other people. It's about how you treat yourself and how hard on yourself you are. It's about your self-confidence (or lack thereof), and level of insecurity. It's about your directness and ability to be forthcoming (or lack thereof). It's about your ability to coax other people to get to the point. It's about your ability to get out of conversations that you don't want to be in. It's about your ability to handle interruptions and distractions. It's about your level of niceness and accommodation with others. It's about the level of drama that you like to have in your life and your level of proactivity, or if you prefer the excitement of being reactive. It's about your level of feeling the need to have everything perfect. And it's about your ability to ignore the noise and keep your mind focused on what's most important.

I will be the first one to tell you that time management is frustrating. Why? Because we have more to do than time to get it done in. Have you met anybody who has more time than things to do? Maybe in fantasy. I once met someone who told me her fantasy was that cloning technology was fully implemented. She said she needed five of herself. She wanted to have a daily morning delegation meeting to give out the assignments to her clones. Then she was panicked because she didn't have enough outfits for all of them. Then she asked me if the clones could be a younger, thinner, more attractive version of herself! But in the real world, the concepts of time management are easy to say and simple to grasp, but not easy to implement. It takes some effort and dedication on your part. This is hard for people.

One of the realities of our existence is that it is temporary. It will come to an end at some point and you will expire. The only question is when and how. I believe we need to be cognizant of this more often. If you don't know how many days you have left, does it make any sense to spend them feeling guilty and overwhelmed?

1. You'll Never be Finished Anyway

Sadly, many people keep themselves going and going in a vain attempt to reach a place that doesn't exist. That place is, "being completely finished" with nothing else left to do. The reason why many people have trouble sleeping is that even though they are physically in bed, mentally they are still not finished, and thoughts of the things still left to do are regurgitating in their mind. Balanced people accept the fact that they will never be completely caught up and don't get themselves all frazzled and worked up trying to.

Even though we know there is a limit to what we can accomplish in one day, we often set unrealistic expectations for ourselves. When we can't accomplish everything on our "to-do list," we berate ourselves for not working hard enough or fast enough. Many of us live with a constant sense of guilt that we didn't accomplish enough, no matter how unrealistic our expectations were in the first place. But do you realize that if you did everything that needed to be done in your life in one day, you wouldn't be a human being? You'd be a superhero.

Our inability to live up to the superhero image keeps us feeling like we're always one step behind. Letting go of this image is the first step in setting realistic expectations for ourselves. Start to let go of your superhero tendencies by recognizing that there is only so much any one person can do in one day. Acknowledge that you have limits, and that pushing yourself beyond your limits will only lead to frustration and exhaustion. We also must accept what we are—human beings. Too few people do this.

The next thing you can do is simply declare yourself "done" on a daily basis. You firmly resolve that after a certain point or time of day, you're not going to attempt anything else and will not do anything of substance. This is an extremely freeing exercise that allows you to recharge your capacities and gives you more balance. "Hey, it's 7:30 p.m. and I'm done for today." I'm reminded of Richard Carlson's phrase, "When you die your inbox still won't be empty." Surrendering to the reality that you'll never be finished takes the pressure and strain off. You can fight reality if you'd like, but it's one of the quickest ways to make yourself ill.

We all know that life is temporary, but sometimes we forget that we don't know when our last day is going to be and how many moments we have left. Since we don't know, one of the most important things has got to be being fully present in the moments of life and enjoying each step along the way—not getting everything done. Remember that even though you will never be finished, you decide when you are done on a daily basis. Lastly, remind yourself that there has to be a reason why we are called human "beings" instead of human "doings."

2. I've Got 1440, You've Got 1440, We've All Got 1440!

What do I mean by 1440? Minutes, when the 24 hours in a day is multiplied by the 60 minutes in an hour. Time is the great equalizer. It doesn't matter how wealthy you are, how organized you are, or how wonderful you think you are, we all have the same amount each day to work with. Unfortunately, you can't buy any more time. We don't all have the same amount of money or status to work with, but we all have the same number of minutes each day to work with. The only difference is how we choose to budget them.

Those minutes just tick away. It's relentless and there's nothing we can do about it. It's also neutral and non-personal. They are what they are and they do what they do. We might as well choose in advance what we will be focused on while time moves on.

Hopefully we all sleep around eight hours so we subtract 480, which gives us 960 waking minutes to work with. I have met people who say they take their children's Ritalin pills that aren't prescribed for them and claim they only need to sleep four hours a night, but that's not healthy.

Thinking about it this way is inspiring and gives you a sense of control. This helps me create a sensible budget for my remaining time. Most of us would have 480 minutes at work and then 480 personal minutes either before or after work.

Now of course there is going be a lot of excess fat here and a lot of downtime when you're in between tasks. I don't budget for all of it—that would be exhausting. I just budget for a small percentage—developing the offense and working on things that will move me forward to my goals. This is also motivating because if I have 960 minutes that I'm awake or even 480 minutes at work, is there really any excuse why I can't allocate 30 of them to focus on a long-term goal? If I've got roughly 480 personal minutes is there any reason why I can't spend 30 of them exercising?

This philosophy also helps us focus. I think society nowadays is out of control with distractions. Even our television screens have distractions on them with information tickers on the bottom. The technology and multiple devices around us have made it harder to focus on just one thing. But it's essential that we do so. This is where the satisfaction comes from. You want to be able to say to yourself, "I set the goal and I met it. I set the goal and I met it." This provides us with

Even 90 minutes of totally focused work time, where your mind is immersed in what you're doing and not following distractions, is probably more than a lot of people get each day. I use a stopwatch to help me, and I only allow the stopwatch to run when I'm 100% focusing on what I set out to do. If for some reason I'm distracted, I stop the clock. Having to take this extra action gives me a chance to consider the decision—am I going to do this or am I going keep going? It also helps with self-discipline to know that I didn't cut any corners. I did what I set out to do.

Now we're talking about things that we can get a handle on, concepts that we can grasp. Items that are under our control. There are so many things in life that we're powerless over. So many folks feel out of control because they're trying to control external things that they have no power over. Can you control your focus? Not for 480 minutes. But can you control it for 150, two and a half hours?

3. Offense Versus Defense

"It's not enough to be busy, so are the ants. The question is, what are we busy about?"— Henry David Thoreau

"Until you value yourself, you won't value your time. Until you value time, you will not do anything with it."—M. Scott Peck

A better way to think about your day and daily time allocations is offense and defense. Offense means you're doing what you would like to do, what's on your agenda, the things that are on your list. A sports analogy would be when a football team has the ball and is running its pre-scripted plays.

Defense would be when you're reacting to what's happening around you. The football analogy would be the defense doesn't know what the offense is going to do, so it must react to what's happening once the ball is snapped. Not all defense is bad. It may be a core part of the mission of your job: to provide service and solve problems that are presented to you.

When I was a manager of provider relations at an HMO, much of my day was spent being on the defensive, reacting to problems and complaints that providers had or helping the people that worked for me with issues that arose. The job was generally 80% defense and 20% offense. That was nothing to feel bad about since that was the nature of the job, as it was considered a service position. In fact, problems with providers could be viewed as opportunities to strengthen the relationship by successfully solving them. It was important for me to acknowledge this reality, not fight it and make myself crazy about it.

However, I had to prioritize and defend my 20% of offense time. It's so easy to stay in a frantic defensive mode with the mindset of, "I have so much to do, I have so much to do." That 20% of my day was roughly 90 minutes. I had to set boundaries around this. I had to make sure it happened. This is the essence of time management. This is where the sanity and sense of control is found.

Regardless your role, there must be some time carved out for offense each day since that's where we make sense of things. Even if you work at a call center, or your job is to only answer incoming calls. There are organizations where they rotate covering for each other so someone could be off the phones to work on something proactive. It may be helpful to check your job description or ask for some clarity from your leaders.

To create your offense ask yourself, "What would you like to have happen? How would you like things to go, or what would you like to accomplish? What are some of your long-term goals?" What are you going to be hit with next month or what is down the road that will be coming due?

Your offensive plan for the day may just be that you want to focus for 30 minutes on two projects or situations. In many cases, you may not complete them, but focusing on it for 30 minutes will move the ball forward. Normally after spending 30 minutes on something it no longer feels as daunting.

Many people feel that all they do each day is put out fires. There's not much of a sense of accomplishment in that. There could be some joy if you feel fulfilled by helping others. However, many times there is guilt and regret for other things that you haven't gotten to, which contributes to stress. One manager at a company where I was doing an internal time management training memorably told me, "Kevin, I don't need any more firefighters, I need a fire-preventer. I would love someone who can anticipate and resolve things before they descend into crisis mode."

So, how much time do you typically spend on offense each day? If you don't think you can, try coming in earlier when your workplace is quieter or hide somewhere where you can't as easily be found and interrupted. Sometimes it is so easy to get drawn into the busywork and we can feel compelled to work on certain matters. A part of effective time management is testing your assumptions and theories.

What do you think would happen, would the earth stop spinning if you make yourself unavailable and focused on a long-term goal for a while? Can you aim for at least 45 minutes each day? It feels much better to be investing your time as opposed to spending it.

4. Stop Saying, "I don't have the time!"

The more I say "I don't have the time," the worse I feel. The more out of control and guilty I feel. It is one of the realities of life that I don't have time for everything. I do, however, have the time for any one thing—if I decide it's important enough—just not for every thing. No one does. You'd have to be a superhero with special powers.

Therefore, the wording that you use with yourself and others is crucial. We have to continually remind ourselves that it's always a choice. I can't do it all, but I have to pick and choose my battles.

Too many people don't honestly assess where their time goes. You can't complain that you don't have time to get your homework done if you don't honestly acknowledge that you spend two hours playing video games or on social media. I've seen statistics that indicate that the average Facebook visit is 45 minutes. The truth can hurt and the stopwatch doesn't lie. A hidden camera wouldn't lie either, and would be extremely accurate and an eye-opening experience, especially if there was several days of data, but is not realistic (and seems creepy).

Don't reinforce something that you don't want to be true. Since we become what we think about, we must be very careful what we allow our mind to dwell on. You may not have enough time. But join the club, no one does. Why make yourself feel all frazzled about it? Are you acting like a modern martyr? Do you want people to feel bad for you? Does this really work for you to get attention?

5. Even at the Happiest Place on Earth

A few years ago, my family and I went to Disneyland in California for two days. The kids were wild with anticipation! We had a fun time and created wonderful memories; it also taught me an important life lesson.

On the first day, everyone was raring to go. We wanted to go on as many rides as possible. We entered the gates and went right through Main Street USA to the first ride that the kids wanted to do, which was Autopia.

And then we waited. And waited. And waited. It was probably 45 minutes until we got to the ride, but the ride was fun and no one's enthusiasm was dampened. But it became clear to my wife and me that we had to do something.

We decided to pull up the park map and huddle with the kids. We had to break the news to them that with those lines we weren't going to able to cover all of the park. Of course, they didn't want to hear this.

Then we learned that the park provides you with a time manage- ment tool. Several of the more popu- lar rides offer a fast pass system where you are given a pass for that ride. The pass tells you to return at a later time window, usually beginning 90 minutes after you get the pass, to avoid most of the line during that timeframe. But they don't let you run around the park

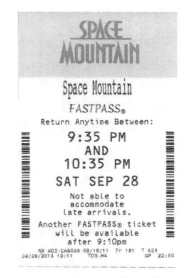

getting several fast passes, you can only get one at a time and it tells you on the pass what time you're eligible to get another one.

This forces you to create a game plan and a strategy for the day. Since you can only get one at a time, while you're waiting for your pass to become eligible, it's smart to wait in a regular line for another attraction. Preferably this should be one that doesn't have the longest lines or doesn't use a fast pass. Then, before you go on the ride that you have the pass for, it's a good idea to get your next pass, so some of that time will tick away while you're on your ride.

They resisted at first, but we got them to come up with a list of which attractions they wanted to do the most. Then we had to look at the map to create the order of attack. We had to consider which ones were closest together, offered fast passes, and had the longest lines. There are a couple that the kids wanted to do multiple times, so we would set those aside for first thing in the morning the following day, before the crowds got big.

The biggest reason why I wanted them to choose was so at the end of the day they wouldn't be disappointed. If one of them said after the fact, "Wait a minute, we didn't get to do ride A," then I could say, "Well remember, we chose to do ride B instead." I also think that looking back, this will probably be the first experience that they'll remember having to manage their time and learning the lesson that you can't do it all and therefore have to make choices.

For me, it was a good reinforcement that even while on vacation at Disneyland, we still have to manage our time and come up with a plan for the day. I think part of me thought I should get a break from that since I was on vacation. I also realized I was associating planning too much with work, as if it were a chore.

But there's no need to stress about it, I shouldn't see it as a punishment and we should all just accept it as a reality of life. Since there is more to do than time to get it done in, one of the worst habits is to simply show up to work in the morning and just do "whatever," meaning not having a specific plan of action. Or just turn on your email and start to read your messages and think you'll figure it out from there.

There's enough guilt in this world, so everyone needs to have a plan, so that at the end of the day they can feel good about themselves. If you don't have a plan, you won't get the satisfaction of meeting realistic objectives and you'll just float around to the wheel that squeaks the loudest. It's also too easy to invent things to do to avoid doing what you don't want to do.

We've got to be able to say, "Wait a minute, before I get started here in this craziness what should be my key objectives for the day?" Then, realistically how long is each one going to take? What should the order of attack be? Which ones ought I tackle first? What resources (like a fast pass) and people might be available to help? For some people, the busier they are, the more they think they had better get started quickly. But the busier you are, the more you need to stop before you begin and rationally think things through. Once you start the day it's hard to stop and think about planning. What's even better is to plan for the next day before you leave work, so hopefully thoughts about work won't interfere as much with your evening personal time.

Don't forget, you can also be planning and scheduling fun. It could be a typical weekend, and you can ask yourself what would be the most enjoyable items to do. This can help you avoid being sucked into an endless to-do list and create more balance in your life by scheduling time to have fun.

I can't come into work and just do whatever, just like I can't

,

arrive at Disneyland and just start to walk around and do whatever. I've got to plan. I've got a look at the lengthy line for a ride and ask myself, "How long will I be in that line, and is the enjoyment of the ride going to be worth it?"

6. Do you Have a Minute?

Isn't this one of the most dreaded questions in the workplace? Some people probably have this thrown at them so much that they hear it in their head when trying to sleep. With some people, we know it's never going to be a minute. It's really going to be closer to a half hour—if we allow it. Some folks are repeat offenders and seem as if they always need our attention and time. However, some people rarely come to us and when they do, we truly want to help them. Sometimes it can be an opportunity to build relationships.

For our purposes, we'll call the person who approaches us the "seeker."

The bottom line is, sometimes we can give the seeker what they need and sometimes we can't. It's a matter of determining what's more important. Therefore, it may not be a simple yes or no answer.

Besides, saying "no" may sound harsh. But responding yes when you're really need to say no does no one any good since you'll not only feel resentful and stressed, you're not able to fully focus on what the seeker is saying.

So, what we need is more information. We need to triage and decide if we are going to stop what we're doing and give the seeker our attention, or if we are going to ask the seeker to come back later (or perhaps go elsewhere) to find what they are seeking.

The best way to do this is to turn this around and throw a question back at them. However, a very specific question. Now, the question would not be, "What do you need?" If you ask them that, then the gates are open and you'll be knee-deep into the interruption.

What you want to do is bring up the amount of time the seeker thinks they need and get a quick summary of what they are seeking. I do mean a quick summary. You also want to establish how much time this is going to take, and the possibility of redirecting them or having them come back later.

Here are some responses I recommend to the question, "Do you have a minute?"

- How much time do you need?
- How much time do you need, and please give me a quick high-level summary.
- How much time do you need, but please know that I have a hard stop in five minutes, so please give me a quick summary.

Now we're talking about time; talking about how much time this is going to take. Not just the substance of what the seeker needs. We're trying to weigh both sides, what they seek and what you have available. We're respectful of both parties. But most importantly, we're leaving open the possibility of having them come back, setting a boundary, and addressing the amount of time this conversation is going to take.

Now, after you've received the quick summation from the seeker, if you're not going to redirect them elsewhere, then you need to respond with the results of your triage.

If what they need is more important than what you're currently doing, then obviously, you'll stop and take the interruption. If it can wait, or if it's going to take longer than the current time you have available or if it's not as important as what you are currently doing, then you're going to set a time boundary. The time boundary could be something similar to this:

"Listen, Kevin. That is important. Realistically, it's going to take around twenty minutes. I have an opening at 2:00. Can you come back then?"

If the seeker is your boss or someone who is at a higher level in the organization, you might want to say something similar to the following:

"Right now I'm working on something important. Could I get back to you at 2:00, or do you need me to stop what I'm doing now?" Sometimes pushing it back on people and asking, 'Do you need me to stop what I'm doing now?" makes them think a little bit. I think people realize that we all have things we're juggling, so it puts the onus on them.

We should also mention the people that approach us and simply want to socialize about non-work related topics. This is normal and has some benefits of socialization and stress reduction. However, this can easily consume a significant amount of our time in the workday. Most people would be quite surprised if the amount of time spent socializing was accurately recorded on a weekly basis. I don't know why it's so difficult for people to simply say to a colleague, "Listen, can you come back at lunch, or can we talk after lunch?" Or, "Sorry, right now I'm trying to focus on something, can we talk later?" I think too many people are concerned that they will come across as short or rude.

We need to let this go and put ourselves first more, especially for the repeat offenders, who for whatever reason really seem like they need someone to talk to or simply need attention. Getting dragged into conversations with someone for fifteen minutes at a time adds up to over an hour per week that could be better allocated elsewhere.

Yet again, it's best to stop thinking and saying that you don't have the time. You have the time. It's a matter of making choices about what's more important.

"So, do you have a minute?" Consider what the answer could cost you. Of course, you have a minute, though perhaps not for the person in front of you, and not right now. The challenge is handling that in a professional manner. A huge part of effective time management is professionally managing the expectations of those around you. It's not easy to have these conversations and set these boundaries, but it so worth it.

7. Ideally Versus Realistically

This mindset of ideally versus realistically is so helpful to keep in mind—for both your own life and when interacting and negotiating expectations with others.

It takes the pressure off to remind yourself that there are many ideals in life that most people would agree would be wonderful. It would be great if we had a magic wand that we could use to make things the way we'd like them to be. The people around us would also be the way we'd would like them to be. But it's just not realistic, and it's not real.

Ideally, you could get all caught up with nothing else left to do. Ideally, things would always go according to plan. Ideally, the people around you would be reasonable, cooperative and you'd see eye to eye with them.

The reality is that our resources and our time are limited, and we don't have control over most things in life. The things we would like to do and accomplish can be limitless. So, before we take something on or make decisions, we have to ask ourselves if we're chasing an ideal, and what the reality of that situation will be.

Last year, my family and I were thinking of going on a long car ride from Boston to Washington DC for a weekend of sightseeing. Ideally, that would be a great time, but realistically, I had to remind myself that the five of us in a car for that amount of time most likely would be unbearable. With three kids vying for attention and all of the technology and noise, we'd most likely drive each other absolutely nuts. Realistically, it just wouldn't be that enjoyable. Flying—that would be another story.

We've simply got to think more before we take actions or agree to do the things that others ask us to do. Being unrealistic is just setting yourself up for failure and is one of the quickest ways to cause yourself to become physically ill.

I remember one day after my wife went to our child's school to meet with the school nurse. She noticed how little support the nurse seemed to have and how challenging her job is. She noticed all sorts of areas where the nurse could use extra help. One of these was the clothing donations that people made for kids who might have an accident at school and need to change. She came home and stated that she was going to go in for a day and help the nurse by organizing all the clothing neatly by age and gender, etc. I thought to myself, "Ideally, that would be great, but realistically, I don't see that happening." I was smart enough to not say it out loud. It hasn't happened, and it's unlikely to ever happen.

I just don't think that we should put pressure on ourselves and make statements like that in the first place about things that aren't likely to come to fruition. You might be eating dinner and the kids ask if they can play Monopoly after dinner, without realizing it's almost seven o'clock. They still have to take showers and finish their homework and you just have to say, "Realistically, there's not enough time for that, not tonight."

This also one of the best phrases to use with the people around you. Since many people are unrealistic, both with themselves and with others, they need to be brought back to reality. This is easier when you validate what they are advocating for by agreeing that you would also like for their proposal to happen, but then, in the same breath, explain why it's not likely.

It simply makes things less of a battle. People get less defensive if you don't immediately shoot down their ideas. The worst things to say to someone are, "You shouldn't feel that way," or, "That's crazy," or, "That's not workable" or, "You're wrong."

It's much easier when you validate their viewpoint by acknowledging their intentions. You may say, "Yes, ideally I would agree with that," or "I would also prefer that were the case" and then in the same breath you make a statement to attempt to steer them back to reality. That may sound like, "However, realistically with the time we have available, I don't see that as possible." This is likely to open the door to a conversation about available resources and deciding what's important, which is a healthy conversation to have for both individuals and organizations. Perhaps Virginia Satir said it best, "Life is not the way it's supposed to be. It's the way it is. The way we cope with it is what makes the difference."

8. Just Say No!

The best word for managing your time and getting your life under control is "no." I don't think we say it often enough. The quickest way to make yourself feel crazy, exhausted and resentful is to say "yes" to things that you really want to say "no" to.

There are lots of people who would just love to waste your time. There are many people who would love to make their priorities your priorities.

To be forthcoming, I think it's important to mention here that there seem to be more narcissists in our society nowadays. You may know some. These are the people who are mostly self-absorbed, entitled, egotistical, vain, arrogant, exploitative or lack empathy. They have no problem at all asking you to do things for them. They are great at manipulation and trying to get you to feel guilty since, of course, the world revolves around them. There is not a thought as to the impact of their request on you and what you have going on; that would require the realization that you haven't been put on this earth to meet their purposes.

Let's call them "askers." Since they don't consider you at all when they ask, you don't have to feel guilty when refusing a request from them. I had a boss like this once, who would simply forget when I had planned vacation days or when I informed him (in advance) of other high-priority items that was I was taking on. He routinely asked me to do things in a non-emotional manner and didn't mind me replying no in a non-emotional manner. I would just say, "You may not realize" or, "You may have forgotten that I have other commitments," or "You may have forgotten that we talked about my vacation. I can resend the email on that if you'd like."

I think one of the best methods for handling the times when you're being asked is to simply state, "Thanks for checking, but that's not going to work for me." If you give a specific reason, they may come up with a specific response to what you say. But a simple, "It's not going to work for me," leaves less wiggle room for them to try to manipulate you. You do not have to elaborate.

For some people, you need to use the broken record technique. This is where you just calmly restate your boundary with them. When they press you on why that's not going to work for you, just calmly reply, "Again, sorry, but that's not going to work for me." You don't want to get sidetracked and go down the road of why it won't work for you. It's also fine to simply say, "Listen, I don't want to get into the details now, but it's not going to work for me."

Sometimes we may even need to say to someone, "What part of this aren't you getting? The N or the O because I can spell it out for you." For some people, you may have to name the dynamic, describing what the conversation is like when you think they're attempting to be manipulative. You may say something similar to, "You wouldn't be trying to make me feel guilty, would you?"

There are also more politically correct ways to say no which may be more useful in the workplace. Another technique is instead of saying no, say "Yes, as soon as (state your requirement)." For example, "Yes, I can help you with that as soon as you can find someone to take this other item off my plate," or "Yes, I can help you with that as soon as you can find someone else to cover my other responsibilities." Or "Yes, I can help you with that as soon as you get me the background items that will be needed for it." When I worked in an HMO and we couldn't pay someone's claim, instead of giving them a flat "no," I'd say, "Yes, we can pay that, as soon as you get us a referral from your primary care physician." For some people, you may just have to say something similar to, "Yes, I can help you with that as soon as hell freezes over!"

It's also important to talk about the consequences, if your boss is asking you to take something on. You can say, "That's fine, I'll take on project A for you, but if I do that I'll have to put project B to the back burner, so I need to make you aware of that and the possible consequences." This also may motivate them to get you some help to take on project B or whatever you need to put on the back burner.

.

9. Create a Stop Doing List and Start Making Some Cuts

"If you want something new, you have to stop doing something old."
- Peter Drucker

Just about all of us would be relieved and have more breathing space by making some cuts in our lives. We only get our time in life under control to the extent that we cut out the lower level activities, the things that are not enjoyable or moving our lives forward, and things that are not the best use of our time. There are also items that deep down, we probably do out of guilt and they cause us some angst. It makes a real difference to think about all these items and create a stop-doing list, which in many ways is more impactful than a to-do list.

The bottom line is we can't do it all. There are more things to be done, and potential things to be done, than time to get them done in. There's a limit. A cap. Trying to fight that reality is fruitless.

As you ask yourself about those items you want to cut out to give yourself more breathing space, it's best to ask quickly and answer quickly, within a second or two. If you make it longer, it's more likely that you'll talk yourself out of it and go around in circles.

The most challenging cuts are the things that we do for other people or organizations on an ongoing basis that we need to get out of and stop doing. It takes a difficult conversation to set this new boundary. This can cause stress and anxiety. The pain/pleasure spectrum comes into play here. We always move away from things that we perceive as painful and towards things we perceive as less painful. We have to associate more pain with continuing to do the things we don't want to do, and view that as more painful than the discomfort of the conversation in which you declare that you'll no longer be doing it.

One good way to break the news to somebody of your new strategy is to say, "I've been doing some thinking and reevaluating. I know in the past I've always done this for you, but moving forward, this is going to have to come from somewhere else and will no longer be my responsibility." If they push back it's best to just hold your ground and keep restating, "Sorry, that doesn't work for me anymore." You may worry about the state of your relationship with this person but I think we need to be more forthcoming and start putting ourselves first more often. I think there are more people who put others first than the opposite. There are also more people who do a better job of taking care of others and need to start taking care of themselves than the opposite.

It's even easier and just as impactful to start outsourcing or delegating items. There is also a time/money spectrum in life. In the different times and stages of life we have more time than money, at other points we have more money than time. Sometimes it's worth spending some money to have others do things for you so you can gain more time for the things that are really important.

I still vividly recall the day around fifteen years ago, when I was determined to save some money and change the fuel pump on my Saturn, by myself. This was after some frustrating and expensive repairs. I had my YouTube videos and a repair manual with pictures. What could go wrong? The fuel pump was inside the gas tank. So, I went to a junkyard and had them remove a comparable gas tank from another Saturn. I backed the car up onto ramps so I could get access. It took the entire day, but I persevered and successfully made the repair with no complications or injuries. I was proud of myself and really thought it was an amazing accomplishment. This wasn't just changing the oil.

At dinner, I was telling my wife about the work and the $300 I'd saved. Unfortunately, I didn't get the response I thought I would. She seemed surprised and asked, "You spent all day on that? What if you spent that time marketing and securing more speaking engagements? Wouldn't that be worth more than $300?"

Upon reflection, although it was satisfying to repair the car myself, she was right. It wasn't that smart and really wasn't the best use of my time. I decided that I need to cut out the auto repair part of my life. I also needed to cut out making travel arrangements, as that can get obsessive. The travel agency does that for me now.

What could you outsource in your life? What could you pay someone else to do? Could you hire a cleaner to clean the house?

Could you hire a teenager to do some paperwork or administrative work for you? Could you find someone online for certain random assignments? Could you use a delivery service for your grocery shopping? I recently ran into a clothes cleaning company that has a pickup and delivery service right from your house.

The stop-doing list is so exciting. Write one today!

10. Interruptions

Interruptions are a huge issue that's on everyone's mind. We are all faced with so many potential distractions throughout the day that can easily throw us off track. It takes longer than you realize to get back to what you were doing before the interruption.

The mistake is taking every interruption and distraction. You can't get rid of all of them. Of course, some interruptions you have to just take, depending on who it is and the situation. If it's someone who's at a higher level than you in the organization or an important customer, then most times you'll have to stop what you're doing and pay attention.

On the flip side, some of them are foolishness and just aren't worth your time. To some of them we need to just say, "Sorry, I just can't help you." I can't accept the mindset of, "I get interrupted all the time and there is nothing I can do about it." If you can incrementally reduce them, even by a small percentage, that is helpful.

There are things that you can do and things that you can say that will help reduce interruptions. It's nice to be a nice person, as long as you're not too nice. If you're too nice, you're likely to struggle with this. I think in the workplace we have to be professional but we can't be overly polite or overly friendly because you'll get very little done. Imagine how ridiculous it would be if you made eye contact and acknowledged every person that walked by your workspace. But there are some people that feel obligated to do so. Some people worry that if they don't they'll be perceived as being unfriendly or others will think they're angry with them. We have to figure out what being too nice costs us to help us move past it and more vigorously defend our time.

I think everybody realizes that we all have other things going on, but a big part of time management is professionally managing other people's expectations of you. You have to be very careful. You don't want to set that expectation of stopping every time someone comes in or set an expectation that you're going to reply to all e-mails within a few minutes.

In order to defend your time, you can't make it too easy or inviting for potential interrupters to just come in to your workspace and get your attention. I've seen many people who put piles of papers on the empty chairs in their workspace to make it harder for interrupters to sit down. It also helps if you stand up when someone enters your workspace as you ask them what they need.

Rearranging the furniture and the direction you face while you're sitting can also have a huge impact. I've had success in suggesting to people who assist coworkers, to change their process. Their desk used to face outwards towards the hallway and people used to walk by and describe the issues they need help with. Some of these folks loved to hear themselves talk and it was difficult to get out of these conversations. They decided to turn their desk and computer against the wall and created a new system, with a wooden inbox on the desk with a large sign that reads, "Please write down your issues and put them in the box. I will get to them and will ask you if I need any clarification."

Creating and posting signs in general can be a great idea. One manager, who I met in a federal agency, was frequently interrupted by her staff asking her questions, and found that she reduced interruptions by posting a sign that read, "Tell me where you've looked already." It's human nature to go to the area of least resistance and easiest source to find the answer. But the manager realized part of her job to is to help develop her staff, and to teach them how to find the answers to their own questions. Therefore, she can't be the first stop—she has to be a stop later down the line, after they have done their part of the legwork. "Tell me where you've looked already," has really worked well. Another system is to have a "frequently asked questions" resource available to all employees on a shared drive, where they can easily look up information. Another easy adjustment, if you have people coming to you sporadically but consistently with questions, is to ask them to hold their questions until the end of the day, or lunchtime, and bring them to you all at once.

Another way to reduce your interruptions is to change your systems, policies, or procedures. My children's school system is a great example of this. They used to frequently have parents coming throughout the day to drop off items that the children forgot. Many of these items were non-essential. They would have to repeatedly open the doors to the building, then the parents would often want to talk to the office staff and this gets everyone off track. Some would demand that the item be delivered to their child's classroom while they wait. Some had no awareness of the effect that this interruption would have on classroom learning. The school system came up with a new policy which was you have a two-hour window in the morning to drop off items. There's an outer door and an inner door. They only buzz you into the outer door, not the inner door. You drop the item(s) off in the lobby in a basket and put the child's name on the item. You don't get all the way in the building to the office. Then there are display moni- tors throughout the school where they post the names of children who have items waiting for them in the pickup area. It's up to the child to know to look at the monitors. They also advise the parents not to drop off homework children forgot, as that is their responsibility and they have to deal with the consequences. It works out great and everyone is breathing a sigh of relief on how this constant stream of interruptions has been stopped.

If you work in a department that services or supports people, you could create a new system of taking turns covering for each other so at least at some point during the day, each person can spend some focused time on long-term goals, knowing they won't be interrupted.

Another thing you can do, which is underutilized, is to hide somewhere for a specific timeframe, also known as "going dark." I think we frequently overestimate how indispensable we think we are. You might make yourself unavailable for forty-five minutes, work at an alternate location, or in an empty conference room, or use a mobile device to get some work done. If you find it hard to focus in your usual workspace, any one of these are good habits to develop.

I've seen organizations that recognized how much of their employees' productivity is hurt by interruptions, create a culture of making a game out of minimizing them. There could be funny hats that you can wear, that you call a "thinking cap" that gives a signal that you're not to be approached or interrupted unless there's an emergency. If you find yourself distracted by noises around you and your workspace, headphones could be an option. If that's not accepted in your organization's culture, I'm a big fan of wax earplugs, they are not so visible as they are light in color and you can get them into your ear canals so they are barely noticeable. This cuts down the noise tremendously. Some people are just inconsiderate and some people don't realize how loud and obnoxious they can be. But what you can do that's under your control is find a way to minimize that noise.

The reality is that some people are attention seekers or else seeking external validation. There are also more people with ADD than we realize who are seeking out distractions. Their brains are looking for stimulation and have a novelty bias that causes them to be bored with their current work and look for that next interesting thing. These folks would love to talk to you and just keep you occupied.

The questions to ask yourself are, "Is this interruption more important than what I'm currently doing? Really? Honestly? How difficult is it going to be to get back to what I was doing? Will this help me avoid something else?" Sometimes I love interruptions because getting sucked into it helps me avoid something that I don't want to do.

One good way to minimize the length of the interruption is to say to the interrupter shortly after they appear, "Listen. I just want to let you know that I have a hard stop at 2:00 p.m." A hard stop means the conversation is going to be over. "I'm just setting that expectation up front, and I wanted to let you know." For the people that just want to socialize with us, I don't understand why not enough people simply say, "Please, I don't mean to sound rude, but could we talk at lunch? I'm occupied with something right now." Or, "Listen, I'd love to talk to you more, but could we do it at lunch?"

Remember, the issue is not that there is people that want to interrupt us, it's that we accept the interruption. It's not that we have all these emails in our inbox, it's that we choose to read them.

11. Just Coming In and Doing "Whatever"

"To choose time is to save time."—Francis Bacon

One of the biggest mistakes people make with managing time is not having a realistic plan of action for each day. There are some people who just come in and check their messages, and figure they'll just take it from there. As soon as you open your e-mail, you're on the defensive because all those messages are the offense. They're problems. They're things that are asking for responses. Or, people will just check in with others to see what they have going on and then the squeaky wheel gets the grease, or they'll find something to do to avoid doing what they don't want to do. Just starting the day and doing "whatever" can be a devastating error. It keeps you feeling frazzled and unfulfilled.

Mick Jagger would tell us, "I can't get no satisfaction." Many of us don't find any satisfaction because we have no plan in place that's going to give us any. Where's the satisfaction at the end of the day, feeling like you just put out fires? The real satisfaction comes from crossing things off, from the progressive realization of worthy goals and objectives. Setting a goal and meeting the goal, setting another goal and meeting the goal, this satisfies. When I cross things off my list, I like to be overly dramatic and make a grunt sound as if I'm lifting heavy weights. It's nice to be able to hang my hat on these victories. To have a realistic plan that we can feel good about at the end of the day is the best thing. "Yes, I got this done!" That's what pumps me up. I feel better if I say, "Okay, I spent an hour on marketing. I spent an hour on my new book."

Sometimes the most profound things are the simplest. In our complicated society, I think most of us would be well served trying to make and keep things simpler.

Many of us struggle with our ability to focus and we tend to allow ourselves to get thrown off track too easily. Having a solid plan helps with this, it keeps you on your agenda more consistently. It's also vital to get you back on track after you've been interrupted. I can't tell you how many times I've been interrupted and pulled off something and afterwards thought, "What was I doing?" Then I figure it out by looking at the plan and saying, "Oh, that's what I'm doing."

When creating the plan, you've got to have your course set for the day, before you begin it and immerse yourself in the work. Once you start it's unlikely that you'll be able to pull yourself out. You won't be able to step back and have the perspective to develop a well-thought-out time allocation for that day. Once you commence your daily battle, the adrenaline starts pumping, and you can get into the fight or flight mode, which results in less blood to your brain to be able to make well-reasoned and wise choices. It's also too easy to invent things to do to avoid what we don't want to do. The busier you are, the more things you think you have on your plate, and the more you think you don't have the time to do them. This is why you need to calmly step back before you begin and plan out the best way to tackle things. You also might discover there are other people and resources that may be able to help you or a more efficient order to address what's on your plate.

Ideally, it's best to make your plan at night before you leave work or shut work down for the day. Have your plan for the following day ready to go so you can hit the ground running the next morning. It also helps you to find more balance in your life to not to have to think so much about work during your personal time, when work is supposed to be over. Imagine if we are paid, not for the hours we are physically at work, but the hours we mentally thought about work? Wouldn't we be wealthy?

So, when creating your plan ask yourself what would you like to have happen? What would be satisfying and make me you feel good? What would excite you when you go through your day? Think of something that's not due imminently but is on your plate. Maybe something that is two to three months out. Think how good it would feel just to spend forty-five minutes on that item tomorrow.

Or, you may realize that you're probably going to have a crazy day and you'll only be able to spend thirty minutes total on something proactive. Or, the plan may be just to rest and recharge for several hours.

The big thing is to choose it in advance, as much as possible. Then just about anything's okay. We need to do this because we have more to do than time to get it done. Our time is limited. We only have 1440 minutes a day. I think it's better to plan in terms of minutes that you will focus on things as we have more control over that. So, if you know the day is going to be nutty, just accept the fact that it's going to be a thirty-minute day, since are there a lot of things on your plate. It's imperative not to feel bad or guilty about it.

If we had unlimited time it wouldn't matter. Just like if we had unlimited money it wouldn't matter how you spent it. Well, time is money and money is time. Choosing how your money is going to be spent in advance means you'll save money. To choose how your time will be spent in advance means you'll not only save time but you'll feel better about things and feel as if you have more control over your life. You'll be able to sleep better at night. If you don't choose in advance you won't get that feeling of accomplishment and sense of satisfaction. You won't be able to physically cross things off a list.

So, make the plan and then work the plan. Tell yourself, "I've made the plan. I'm going to work the plan. I'll keep looking at this. I'll keep going back to it. This is my rock." I think you either have a plan for the day and for the week—a realistic plan—or you plan to fail and be upset.

12. Schedule Meetings With Yourself

One of the hardest things to do with time management, but one of the best things to do, is to schedule your time to be on the offense. This means being proactive by focusing for a set amount of time on something that's not urgent, and nobody is asking for. It's not yet a crisis or emergency, but spending a half hour on it today will help it avoid becoming a fire that you'll have to fight next month. Or, think of a long-term goal, or something you've been procrastinating about.

I call it a meeting since you give it the same respect that you'd generally give a meeting that you attend. Especially with your superiors. You FOCUS on the meeting topic. You "monotask." You're not being disruptive and taking calls while sitting in the meeting room or checking your email (unless you're hiding a mobile device). Isn't the reason why many folks complain about meetings not allowing them to get done what they need, is because they can't do those other things while they're in the meeting?

So, what you do is schedule a meeting with yourself for a set amount of time to focus on a specific agenda topic. You put things away that would be distracting or disruptive, and close other computer programs, such as your messaging and email.

To help me focus during my meetings I use a stopwatch, but there are many types of timers available. You may use the Pomodoro Technique. Pomodoro is the Italian word for tomato, and Francesco Cirillo from Italy used a tomato-shaped kitchen timer. However you structure it, the concept of breaking work down into intervals, separated by breaks for your mind to recover, has been proven beneficial. Having a set stop time helps me to avoid any perfectionist tendencies and over-committing to a task. I make a little game out of it. I'll look at a project I'm about to tackle and before I begin I write down a goal time of how many minutes I think it will either take or how many I'm going to allocate towards it now. As the stopwatch is running next to me it serves as my accountability partner. This is even more relevant since I'm my own boss with no one scrutinizing my work and output. The stopwatch doesn't lie. The numbers are the numbers.

When I was in the military, the drill sergeants would always be demanding, "Give me 30," during basic training. I can still hear those words and envision that scene. Back then, they were asking for push-ups, but nowadays I use that phrase to challenge myself for a task. Can I give that task 30? Thirty dedicated minutes?

It works even better if you can remove yourself from your usual work environment, especially if you have coworkers who are likely to interrupt. It can be awkward during this time frame if someone approaches you and you have to inform them that you're in a meeting, especially since you're alone. You may have to explain that it's a meeting between me, myself and I. They may ask you if you regularly talk to yourself.

But seriously, sometimes you just have to think outside the box and find somewhere to hide. It's called going dark, or going off the grid. Available conference rooms are great, or an empty cubicle or any open workspace other than your primary one. I've gotten to know receptionists from companies located on other floors of the buildings I've worked in and they have connected me with vacant, quiet spaces where I won't be bothered. Some airports even have private rooms that you can rent hourly. A lot of organizations now provide their staff with laptops or other mobile devices they can use to accomplish things at locations other than their anchored desktop. If not, print out enough work for forty-five minutes. If your company has some sort of application were everyone's schedule is shared, block off that time as meeting time. No one has to know there is no one else in the meeting with you.

So, the question becomes, when are you most likely to be able to carve out your time to play offense? I think for most people, it's early in the morning before everyone gets in, the phone starts ringing and the nuttiness commences. To get in there and start your day by working on a long-term goal or something that hasn't reached calamity mode yet, is one of the most fulfilling things. The workflow of your organization might be different, so find those times when you are least likely to be interrupted or needed by others.

Doing this helps you feel like you're more in control of your own destiny and pulling your own strings. No matter how arduous the day turns out to be, at least you can feel good about the time you spent on offense and working on your long-term goals. I'd be hard-pressed to find a reason why I couldn't block off at least thirty minutes a day.

After all, what's the one thing in time management that people talk a lot about finding, but never do? I find some when I travel from the East to the West Coast, but for most of us it's elusive? You never find the time. You're never going to find the time to do anything. It's not going to happen. Therefore, what do we have to do? We have to schedule it. Some people say it's most important to prioritize your schedule. I say it's more important to schedule your priorities.

This takes the most self-discipline. Some people need to remind themselves that they aren't working in a medical treatment facility. No one is going to bleed to death if they go dark for thirty minutes, can't be found and don't check their messages. The best characteristic of a good time manager is the mindset of, "I'm not going to be sucked into the day-to-day stuff. I'm going to block off and allocate thirty minutes for this. Unless the building is burning—if the building is burning, let me know. Otherwise, I'll see you in thirty minutes." Try it.

Chapter 6

13. Stupid Meetings

For many organizations, the biggest time-eater is the wasteful meeting. Of course, some meetings are productive and helpful. Some meetings are a good exchange of information and help to build group consensus.

But there are far too many that are just a waste of time. The worst thing about them is the opportunity cost, what they prevent you from doing if you didn't have to attend the meeting. I love this image below from Café Press:

So, what can we do in the workplace about meetings?

First of all, there needs to be an honest assessment of its necessity.

Someone needs to ask the following questions:

- Do we really need to have this meeting?
- What would happen if we didn't have this meeting, what would the consequences be?
- Would the earth stop spinning without this meeting?
- Instead of weekly, could we have this meeting monthly?
- What would happen if we had it via conference call instead of face-to-face?
- Is this is just an informational delivery type of gathering, not a brainstorming session where contribution is needed from attendees?
- Is there a more efficient way for folks to get information on the results of the meeting?
- Could this information be delivered to the attendees in an email or memo?

Another angle to pursue, especially if attempts to stop the meeting are unsuccessful, is to ask if you personally need to attend the meeting.

That may sound something like, "Would it be okay, since I'm not on the agenda (or don't have much to contribute), that instead of attending in person, could I receive a summary of the meeting?" When you're making requests to your superiors regarding these types of matters, it is always better to mention the positives of what you will be able to accomplish in lieu of attending the meeting. You don't want to come across as just complaining or implying that you're overwhelmed.

You want to sell them on the idea that you have better uses of your time that will contribute more to the overall good. So, make it less about you and more about the common objectives that you will be able to work on instead of attending. That might sound something like, "If I didn't have to attend, then I would be able to address that important situation that we discussed yesterday."

However, if the meeting is going to happen, there are several things that meetings need in order to be efficient and effective as opposed to painful.

First of all, you need a leader who is not afraid to lead the meeting. One of the most frustrating things is to be sitting in a meeting that the leader doesn't have effective control over. He or she is letting the attendees go off-track, off-agenda and not keeping things moving and productive. You have to be able to cut people off in an assertive but polite manner. That might sound something like, "Kevin, thanks for your input, and now I'd like to hear from someone else." Or, "Kevin, those are some good points. I don't want to take up everybody's time now during the meeting to address them, but I will chat with you about all of that afterwards."

Another thing meetings need is a clear agenda of what is going to be discussed. If you don't have an agenda it can become a free-for-all, which is devastating to your time management. Taking the time to create an agenda beforehand tells others you care about them and everyone's time is going be respected. This also gives you an opportunity to distribute it to the attendees so they can think about it and be better prepared. If there is information that needs to be absorbed, a pre-read is a good idea, so people will have read and absorbed the information before they attend.

Once you have the clear agenda, the next thing meetings need is a "parking lot" for items that will inevitably come up during the meeting. The phrase "parking lot" is effective because it implies that we're not going down that road now. We are putting that off to the side and we're not giving that topic any traction. That may sound something like, "Thanks for bringing that up, Kevin. That's a good point, but that's not part of the topic for today's meeting, so I'm going to put that in the parking lot to be discussed at another time or at another meeting."

The next thing that meetings need is for start and stop times to be respected by all. This is common courtesy but not always common practice. If not respected, it looks like you don't care, and that you're not aware how your actions affect other people's time. Everyone needs to show up on time. The leader of the meeting needs to make sure it ends on time. If things look like they're not going to end on time, there shouldn't be a problem with anyone speaking up and saying, "Listen, I'm sure everybody's time here is valuable, and I'm sure some of us have made commitments after the advertised end time of this session, so I want to make sure that we bring the discussion back so we can all finish on time." Or, "I want to make everyone's aware that I have a hard stop at_____, so let's do our best to end on time."

The next thing meetings need to be effective is participants who are prepared and ready to go. The agenda needs to be looked at, a pre-read has to be done, and the points they want to make need to be ready to go.

Another thing meetings need to be effective is for people to be succinct and get to the point. Participants who talk in circles need to be prompted by the leader and encouraged to get to the point. It's okay for a leader to interrupt if they justify it with the premise that it's for everyone's collective good that the meeting stays on track, and will end on time. Everyone's time is valuable and needs to be respected.

The last thing that meetings need to be effective is a set of clear takeaways. There's got to be a summary at the end and it should be crystal clear to all the participants what the next steps are and who is taking them.

This may involve an organizational or cultural reflection that needs to take place. Organizations and their leaders have to be cognizant of the number of employee hours that a meeting can consume. A 90-minute meeting with 15 attendees consumes 22 ½ hours of employee time that could be reallocated elsewhere for more vital matters. This type of awareness can be an opening to simply ask the leaders if they would consider alternative suggestions. It never hurts to say, "I've been doing some thinking about the best uses of our time. I didn't realize the effect that these weekly meetings are having and what it's taking us away from." Unfortunately, sometimes meetings are about ego and insecurity. Or, about somebody getting the chance to hear themselves speak and look and feel important or reassert their authority. I think we change culture one conversation at a time. But we must start somewhere.

14. Failure to Communicate

"What we've got here is a failure to communicate. Some men you just can't reach."—Cool Hand Luke

Poor communication is the root cause of so much wasted time and effort. There are six main strategies or areas of communication that have a major impact on time management: Being forthright and candid, clarifying, pushing back, being realistic, asking for help, and status updates.

Being forthright and candid

Since we don't have the ability to read minds, if people aren't forthright or forthcoming, everyone's time gets wasted. We've got to be up front and to the point with others. It refreshing to know where you stand, what you need that you're not getting, what you're getting that you don't want, and what your non-negotiables arc. I've seen friends at a restaurant get a shared pizza with toppings they didn't want because they assumed that's what the other wanted and neither one was forthcoming enough to just come out and say what they wanted. Isn't that crazy?

1. Think of the phrase, "He or she's just not that into you." I think one of the reasons why that book (and movie) were so popular is that it's a breath of fresh air to be forthright and it saves so much time. I can't meet Mr. or Mrs. Right when I'm with Mr. and Mrs. Wrong, so, thank you for saving me three to five years of my life trying to get you to turn yourself around and thinking you'll change and eventually become the person who I think you should be!

2. I prefer the phrase "to be forthcoming" in lieu of "to be honest." Think of what you're implying when you preface statements with, "to be honest." Aren't you implying that sometimes the opposite is true, that sometimes you're not honest?

3. One of my friends, who's an attorney, shared with me one of the best examples of using this strategy. He charges his clients by billable hours and creates and negotiates contracts for them with other businesses. One of his clients is arduous to work with since

too many people in the company have to put their two cents in on multiple minor contract details and changes. It has to rotate among many internal departments that getting them to make a decision and have everyone on the same page is painful. When they were asking him for his estimate on how much the thought it would cost to develop and finalize a contract with a new customer, he told them:

This should cost $20,000.00, but to be forthcoming, you all make things much harder than they have to be and have too many chefs in the kitchen getting involved, so unless you all change your processes there with contracts it takes double the time, so realistically this will cost you closer to $40,000.00.

I loved it! You could argue that why does he care since he's getting paid according to the time he spends, the longer he works on it the more he gets paid. But I think he's acting in the client's best interest. He's saving them money and probably cementing his relationship with them in the long run. Sometimes you've just got to go ahead and say things to people. Saying it also helped his sanity and reduced his frustration level.

Clarifying

Many people do not do this effectively. Isn't one of the biggest wastes of time to do something the wrong way? Because now you have to spend double the amount of time; you have to go back and redo things the right way. Sometimes the instructions aren't clear and sometimes we interpret them incorrectly. We need to clarify and say, "Wait a minute, let me just make sure." Sometimes people won't ask questions because they're afraid how that makes them look. This is unfortunate since we need to ask the five Ws and one H. These are: who, why, what, when, where and how. The answers to these questions are considered basic information-gathering or problem-solving. They are often mentioned in journalism, research, and police investigations. Saying something as basic as, "I want to make sure that I'm getting this correctly, you're saying_____" also helps.

- With managing competing priorities, it's also important to clarify with others why their deadline is what it is, simply because many people cry, Wolf! and overstate the importance of their request. They state they need something several days before it's really needed, just to make sure they get it in time. Some people are overly anxious and overly dramatic. I'm sure you know someone like that. We have to flush them out in order to make good decisions about where our resources should be allocated.

Pushing back

We just can't accept everything that's thrown at us. We need to push back a little, not only to clarify when it's really needed and how important it is, but how it compares to what we currently have going on. This can be difficult, since the person who's asking you to do something (or perhaps trying to dump something on you) might be emotional or in a hurry. Too often, we're too anxious and we agree to things too quickly.

1. When somebody is asking you to do something, I think it's important to ask them, "What's going to happen on your end if you don't get it by Friday? Is the earth going to stop spinning? Is someone going to get hurt? Is this your deadline or is that your customer's deadline? Tell me a little more about what's happening or could happen on your end."

I have an attorney friend and this happens to him quite a bit at his law firm. They would say to him, "We need this contract ready by Friday." He would cramble and get it completed and sent by Friday. But then he would see on the read receipt (which have mixed reviews, but sometimes I like to see when people actually open my e-mail) that they didn't even open it until the following Wednesday. So, they really didn't need it on Friday, did they? That reminds me of the phrase, "Fool me once, shame on you; fool me twice, shame on me." Don't let them fool you twice.

2. To push back further, when somebody is asking you to do something, you should also have a chance to say, "May I just tell you what is on my plate right now? Here are the items, who they have been promised to, and deadlines we've committed to. Now, I'd be happy to help you with your project, but I just need you to tell me which one of these we can either put on the back burner, can wait, or we get someone else to help and take it off my plate." I think most people are reasonable and expect that you have other things that you're juggling. However, we have to communicate this as they may not realize both the quantity of what you already have, and

that it may be more important to the organization than what they have for you to do.

Being realistic

We don't want to overpromise and under-deliver. All that does is disappoint and cause negative consequences for all parties involved.

1. Therefore, reality is exactly the language we should be using when people are either being unreasonable or asking for things that just aren't realistically going to get done in the requested timeframe. You also may need to educate them about what's on your plate and use phrases such as, "You may not realize...," or "Ideally vs. realistically..."

2. That may sound something like, "Ideally, I'd love to get that done for you by Friday. Realistically, I'm probably looking at midpoint next week. I don't want to promise something to you that I can't deliver." You could also add, "You may not realize that I've already promised a lot to so-and-so already this week. Maybe we can find some other resources to help you, but again I don't want to be un-

realistic with you." Here's another version, "Just a minute, let me tell you what I have on my plate. I'm juggling this and that, I want to make sure I can fit this in and make it work for everyone."

3. Sometimes it's important to validate what other people are saying and the urgency they have or how they feel. I'm reminded of the scene in the Apollo 13 film when the ground crew is desperately trying to find the resources to creatively bring the stranded astronauts home. Gary Sinise's character is in the flight simulator going through how he wants to do the power-up procedures. There is tension between him and ground control folks since he keeps insisting on the resources he wants, which they just don't have. Finally, ground control says to him, "You're telling me what you need. I understand that. But I'm telling you what we have to work with. We have to find another way."

4. We as individuals, (and also organizations as a whole), have more to do and things that we'd like to accomplish than we have the resources and time to get done. So, having these collisions of priorities bring heathy conversations. Both parties should be share what they see as the most crucial items to bring to the front burner. If you

Need help making a final decision, the you ought to bring it up the ladder in the organization to get their viewpoint. We just can't passively accept what folks are trying to dump on us, and we can't say things that we just think people want to hear. I'm not saying these conversations aren't difficult or stressful. But they're necessary.

Asking for help

I hate to see people struggling with and suffering in silence. Just to exist as a normal human being requires interaction with other people.

Our connections to others are key, not only to our survival, but also to our happiness and the success of our careers. We are, so to speak, biologically hard-wired for interacting with others, and are thus said to be endowed with a "social brain." People get tremendous satisfaction from being able to help others and to feel needed and appreciated. Some folks are naturally better at some professional skills than others, and we all have unique qualities to contribute. So, there is no need to feel insecure and worry about how we'll be perceived if we ask for help and guidance.

Status updates

What drives so many managers and leaders crazy is when their people keep to themselves how their assignments are going. They may have someone who's working on something with a Friday deadline and they get a sense on Tuesday that they're not going to make it, but the employee just doesn't say anything to let them know. Of course, not until Thursday night. The leaders always say, "If you just would have told me earlier in the week, perhaps we could've done something."

With any of these communication strategies, it's just not enough to say what the strategies are. We have to realistically address the blocks and the mental hang-ups that get in the way of actually having these difficult conversations. I find many of us already know what we need to do, but we can easily talk ourselves out of it. We've got to be mindful enough to be able to notice the thoughts we're having that are getting in the way. Then we have to counter them with more rational thinking.

Another technique to help you get over the block is the five second rule. I don't mean about food and germs. I mean when we know we've got to speak to or set a boundary with someone, go ahead and do it soon as you realize it, within five seconds. That way you don't give yourself a chance to talk yourself out of it. So, if you know you need to make that phone, call go ahead and do it in five seconds of the initial thought, before you talk yourself out of it.

15. What's Your System?

"This constant, unproductive preoccupation with all the things we have to do is the single largest consumer of time and energy."
-Kerry Gleeson

"I never commit anything to memory that easily can be looked up."
- Albert Einstein

In today's fast-paced world, we are inundated with information and distractions. And then we have our busy minds, or monkey minds, with our rapidly shifting internal thoughts. Many of these thoughts are about what we have to do or should to be doing.

Therefore, we all need some kind of a system that works for us. This system has to help our mind to be calmer and clearer and by acting as a master collection bucket for all the significant thoughts that come to mind that we feel we need to take action on.

If we don't have a system, our heads are going to be all filled up and preoccupied with what we have to do. Some people use the phrase, "a lot on my mind," but I like to say it's a lot in your mind that's

Look at the images below of the two heads. Imagine if the dark blotch signified the percentage of your thoughts or consciousness which are dedicated towards what you need to get done. Obviously, the person on the left would have a lot of bouncing thoughts, which makes it difficult to concentrate and focus on just one thing. In fact, the same area of our brain that gets utilized when we are trying to focus also gets utilized when we are trying to remember things. So, the more things you're trying to remember or keep track of, the less you're able to focus. Clearly, you want to be more like the person on the right.

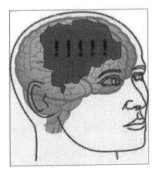 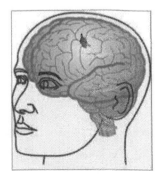

I decided that Albert Einstein was smarter than me, and I'm going to defer to him. He said in the quote above that he doesn't commit anything to memory that easily can be looked up. Our brains are better used for creative thoughts and ideas. There has to be room for thoughts we haven't thought of before, not just this same old

To accomplish this your system has to track what needs to be done and followed up on and make you feel more in control. I don't advocate or sell one particular system. There are so many options and apps out there. Try a few different ones to find one that works for you. Although for years I used to carry a 3 x 5 spiral notebook around with me, (with some corners folded over so I could find my sections on work life, home life, and the next time I would be at a Home Depot) a paper system is mostly obsolete.

I think all the technology in our lives can easily negatively impact us and our ability to be fully present in the moments of our lives. However, we should at a minimum insist that it help to give us a calmer mind by using it as a collection bucket for our thoughts. It's important that your system allows you to view what you enter into it on all your devices—home desktop or laptop, work computer, mobile device, etc. I found that the notes section on the iPhone works well and I dictate items in. I also find it unfortunate when I see people on their mobile devices typing out every character for words instead of using a voice recording feature. If it forces you to practice clear enunciation, then so be it. As I write this I'm not typing on the key-

Evernote and OneNote are also good apps. If you have a Windows product, the Sticky Notes accessory enables you to plaster the electronic equivalent of good old-fashioned Post-It notes all over your desktop. You can use it as onscreen reminders and you can even color code them to help you stay organized.

For family coordination, we are currently using Cozi. The days of a dry erase or bulletin board at home are past us now. There needs to be an online central repository where everyone can enter new events and they can be viewed in real-time. We also like the Cozi feature where anyone can enter items they need at the grocery store so nothing is forgotten when we are at the store and review the app. Many others I know have found that Google Calendar and Tasks work well for them.

Whatever you use, you have to trust it and keep it close by, almost a constant companion. Some of the best things I think about happen at unexpected times. I find for me now as soon as I think it, something that has to be done or a good idea, I have to capture it. I have a pretty pathetic time limit of how soon I'll lose a thought if I don't. So, what is your system that you currently use to track what needs to be done and followed up on? How is that working for you?

16. I've Got a New Message!

It's very easy to do nothing all day but just answer your messages. This is very alluring because our mind has a novelty bias and is always looking for that next shiny thing. However, this is mainly defense since they are asking for responses and taking our mind off track. It's like getting stuck in quicksand.

If you're serious about managing your time and being a highly effective person, you've got to read your messages in chunks. I'm not saying it's easy to do and doesn't take self-discipline, but it's absolutely essential. We have got to tone down the drama, and tone up the sanity.

You've got to remind yourself that you're not working in a medical emergency treatment facility. Nobody's bleeding to death based on your emails. Remind yourself that if there is a real emergency someone will call or come get you.

The first step is you absolutely have to shut down your email program until you consciously choose to check your messages. It shouldn't constantly be running in the background while you're working, even though that's how most people have it set up. Do you really need an alert, ping, chime, flash, or vibrate every time a message comes in? Isn't that hurting you?

If you do allow your messaging accounts to constantly alert you, you'll always be lost in a myriad of stops and starts. There it is, the envelope icon or some message preview flashing on screen, or your all-too-disruptive notification sound. It's just too tempting, so remove the temptation. If you need to do work with the message program, then disconnect from the server so disrupting new messages won't appear.

If we choose a specific time to check our email, we'll have gained specific blocks of time to fully focus, and to be on the offense. You could simply check at the top of the hour, or every half hour. If your work requires it, you could check frequently—but not constantly.

For most folks, three to four times a day should be sufficient. In the meantime, just resist the temptation. Consider the urgency of your typical message, and then you'll understand why some professionals manage to deal with email only a few times a day and still stay fully connected, respond directly to the most important tasks, and get more accomplished every week.

Setting up an automatic email reply is another effective way to reduce your anxiety about your messages and carve out some uninterrupted time for yourself. On busy workdays, even when you're in the office, set up a brief automatic reply that says something along the lines of:

"I've received your message and it is important to me, but I'm trying to get a lot of work done today, so I will only be responding to emails at 10am, noon, 2pm, and 4pm today. If your message is an emergency, please call.........Thank you."

This goes a long way since people aren't going to think you're ignoring them or you're being unproductive.

Again, a major part of time management is professionally managing other people's expectations of you. If you set the expectation that you're going to reply to email quickly, then other people are going to hold you to that.

Remember, messaging makes a wonderful servant but a terrible master. For further reading on this topic, please see: <u>Message Right: Take Control of Your Emails, Texts, and IMs for Maximum Effectiveness and Sanity.</u> By Kevin Stacey, TrainRight Media. ISBN 13: 9780692473290

17. The Killers: Perfectionism and Insecurity

"The problem in my life and other people's lives is not the absence of knowing what to do but the absence of doing it." -Peter Drucker

If you're a perfectionist, you'll spend twenty minutes on something that should only take two. You'll re-read it, rewrite it, replay it in your mind, and go around and around with it. This is so unfortunate. Perfectionism is a futile state of existence that far too many practice. It eats up so much of our spirit of enjoying life. The bar is set so high that it's impossible to reach and you set yourself up for failure and disappointment. Perfectionists also find it very hard to ever have any fun. They can't allow themselves to have fun because they can't stop. They can't stop working because no matter what is they're working on it still could be improved upon, it still could be better, than it currently is.

Insecurity also costs you to so much. It's another huge time and energy waster. You waste so much worrying about yourself and what others think of you. You're way too invested in receiving others' approval and recognition.

There are so many negative manifestations to this I must put them in a list.

The more insecure you are, the more:

- exhausted you are
- quick you are to try and please
- you take on things that are not your job or responsibility
- defensive you are
- you feel the need that you must defend yourself
- easily offended you are
- you take things personally
- you're less open to suggestions
- you're less open to better ways of seeing things or doing things
- you read into things too much
- you simply try too hard
- you're too focused on yourself and self-centered
- you seek attention, positive or negative

- you're too high maintenance and too needy
- you're too dependent and invested in what others think of you
- you think the world is so fascinated with you
- you must post constant updates to social media about your life so others can "like" it
- you can't get over yourself

Back when I was a manager of provider relations at an HMO, I would occasionally travel around with my team members for a day to visit the medical offices that they were servicing. My insecurity would cause me problems since I was too quick to offer my help and direct contact information to the office staff. I would end up being inundated with issues that should have been directed, at least initially, to my team members. They were supposed to be the first line of contact. My job was to step in only if they needed help or if the issue had to be escalated. But when you're insecure you are too quick to try and please, the chain of command breaks down, and you end up taking on other people's work and it's hard for you to backtrack and get out of those situations.

So, that was the issue I needed to work on. All the time management techniques in the world weren't going to work. I can't just say to anybody who's insecure, "You need to set boundaries. You need to say no. You need to start letting go and delegating. You need to stop being sucked into this stuff." They're correct and good things to say, but it's not going to have any impact because just coaching them on what words to say doesn't mean they're going to say them. The root

It's important for people to reflect on why they are the way they are. I think the genesis for these two issues, as most issues, is your childhood. If you felt on some level during your upbringing that you weren't enough just the way you were, or if you didn't feel unconditionally loved for just who you were, challenges occur. This results in you feeling on some level that you needed to strive to achieve things to gain the approval of one or both of your parents. This results in you, aware of it or not, still striving for that external approval into your adulthood and in the workplace.

We must do some honest reflection and ask ourselves who instilled this in us? Which parent or relative was it?

Then we need to give ourselves the acceptance that we just didn't get. We have to learn to like ourselves and accept that we have strengths and weaknesses and we're not meant to be perfect. It's okay to strive for things to be perfect, but we must realize that it's an illusion since we are imperfect beings. We're not meant to be the expert on everything. Yes, it can be improved upon, it could be better, but it is good enough and we are good enough. Done is better than perfect. We have to get to that place called enough.

We then need to pay more attention to what we say when we talk to ourselves. We all have a constant inner dialogue going on. Some people have never left home yet emotionally since they still have a residual self-critical voice from one of their parents instilling destructive criticism. We need to stop the self-destructive thoughts and counter them with realistic and rational thinking.

Most of this is just garbage inside of our heads. When you recognize a thought that you should do something, ask yourself "Is this my expectation or is this the company's expectation? Has it ever been expressly stated to me that the expectation is for me to check my messages at 1:00 a.m.? Is this thought I'm having from the functional self-confident part of me or the dysfunctional insecure part of me?"

We have to heal that child within, and then the adult will emerge.

18. Procrastination

Procrastination is a fascinating form of self-sabotage. One simple way to understand and overcome it is by using the pain-pleasure spectrum. We naturally move away from things that we perceive to be painful and towards things that we perceive to be less painful. Therefore, whatever we dread, we delay, since we associate less pain with delaying the work than doing it. I love the phrase (and book) from Brian Tracy, "Eat that frog" because if the worst thing you have to do on a daily basis is eat a live frog, does it make sense to wait until 5:00 to do it? Because you'll be dreading it all day, along with it distracting you and occupying valuable space in your head. And if you have two frogs to eat, eat the ugliest one or the biggest one first. Then there's nothing left to dread and a big burden is lifted.

My best days are always when I start the progress early. Even if I just spend ten minutes on the most important, but perhaps not the most enjoyable item, before I start clicking around in the typical "click bait" or online news articles or my messages, I feel like I'm getting some momentum and it's going to be a good day.

A good strategy is to use this understanding to start associating feelings of pleasure or a sense of accomplishment with completing something, along with the relief of putting it behind you, and large amounts of pain and discomfort or stress with waiting and delaying. A simple example is our weekly trash pickup, which in our neighborhood is on Monday morning. This is ideal, since we can get rid of all the trash from the weekend's activity right away. Of course, it's not so great on Sunday night, as nobody wants to gather it all and put it in the barrels to be ready to be brought to the curb for the next morning. It's a pain. But waiting until Monday morning to do this is even worse since it's much more chaotic than Sunday night. Everyone is getting ready for school, lunches need to be made, clothes need to be put on, the backpacks readied, and we have to get the kids out to the bus stop on time.

Either way it's painful. There's no way to avoid the pain, but Sunday night is less painful. That's the mindset we need to have. Pain in life is inevitable, but misery is optional. So, which option is worse? We might as well just go ahead and get it over with. I can remember being in grammar school and waiting until the last Sunday before a project was due, rushing and staying up late with an anxious feeling in the pit of my stomach while trying to pull it together. All so unnecessary and all so self-inflicted. Another great reminder is, "Do what you have to do so you can do what you want to do." The Nike Corporation also trademarked one of the best anti-procrastination phrases with, "Just Do It."

What do you have in your life that's painful? What are you dreading doing or delaying on? How's that working for you and how does that make you feel? How do you think it would feel to just start addressing it for fifteen minutes? It never seems as bad once you begin it. When tax season time is approaching and it's time for me to start compiling the information on my business-related travel expenses, it always seems daunting until I actually begin it. I find there is an interesting relationship between the things I'm stressing over and the answer to asking myself, "How long have I actually spent focusing on that item?" This is another reason why I'm such an advocate for using and keeping a stopwatch close by. I can do just about anything for fifteen minutes. I have a goal and I can see that I'm getting closer as the minutes are ticking away.

For the things that appear particularly daunting, ask yourself, "How do you eat an elephant?" It can only be done one way: a bite at a time. Trying to gulp it down in one sitting is asking for severe indigestion. Take it in chunks, pre-defined intervals with some sort of reward you give yourself at the end of the interval. Perhaps something fun or some type of action to take care of yourself.

Procrastination can also have some deeper and more complicated causes. Sometimes procrastination can be a form of self-punishment as it keeps us in a perpetual state of feeling bad about things. This goes back to how we feel this is what we deserve. I think sometimes procrastination is a way that we hold ourselves back from what, on some level, we may not feel we deserve. It can also be a way to protect ourselves from our fear of success. We only allow ourselves to achieve a level that is consistent with our self-image. Some of us need to work on our self-image and ask ourselves some tough questions.

I've seen people have success with speaking directly to their subconscious minds through affirmations, visualization and utilizing hypnosis. As Marianne Williamson says, "Our deepest fear is not that we are inadequate. Our deepest fear is that we are powerful beyond measure. It is our light, not our darkness that most frightens us." Don't let procrastination keep your light dim!

Final Thoughts

Most people don't want to do this. You have to be open minded, since this is very personal. Most people are ingrained in their habits and they do what they do because that's what they are comfortable doing. The difficulty with this topic of time management is that it challenges you to take different actions, make different choices, and have different responses and thoughts than what you're currently having or doing.

To see things differently, communicate differently, set some boundaries with some people, and change the way you talk to the people in your life is difficult.

Even though it's difficult, it is so worth it. Nothing changes if nothing changes. And no one changes anything unless they want to. So always ask yourself what it costs you or will continue to cost you if nothing changes. I encourage you to keep working on it, because you're worth it. Please fill in the next page, the action plan.

Action Plan/ Commitments Page

1.   Based on what I just read, here are the old habits I want to change or eliminate:

_____

_____

_____

2.   Here are the new habits I want to develop:

_____

_____

_____

3.   Who will I ask to help me, and what will I ask them to do?

_____

_____

_____

_____   _____

Signature   Date

About the Author

Kevin Stacey, MBA, is a productivity expert and author who teaches people how to eliminate self-created problems and distractions that impede success. He combines his military background, management training and experience as a healthcare clinician and successful manager at the nation's largest managed-care company to bring experience, wisdom, perspective, and humor to your organization. His programs provide concrete information and practical solutions for business problems. Kevin's knowledge, experience, warm demeanor, and sense of humor create a human connection with individuals that motivates them to make positive changes.

Kevin has a proven record of helping organizations enhance their environment and productivity. From IBM to The New York Times, Ford Motor Company, JP Morgan Chase, Pharmacia, Bayer, Goody Hair Care, United Technologies, Boeing, and Sara Lee, he has worked with the world's best and brightest and studied the effects of self-created problems on organizations and individuals along with the most effective antidotes to combat it. His services help these and other clients achieve increased performance, sales, higher employee retention, greater job satisfaction, and improved service quality.

Kevin's diverse life experiences and achievements include the following:

Professional Speaking and Writing:

- Conveyed his original principles on success to over 60,000 people in 48 states and 4 nations since 1999.

- Author of "MessageRight: Take Control of Your Emails, Texts and IMs for Maximum Effectiveness and Sanity" ISBN 13:9780692473290

- Author of "Mental Toughness: Manage the Clutter to Achieve Success and Peace of Mind," which helps people use mental programming techniques to bring their goals into reality and choose their own attitude regardless of circumstances.

- Contributing author to the "Don't Sweat the Small Stuff Stories" book.

- Member of the National Speakers Association, American Society for Training, and Toastmasters.

Management/Education:

- Earned an MBA with a concentration in healthcare administration.
- Promoted to manager at the nation's largest managed-care company.
- Managed teams of service professionals through the corporate integration following the billion-dollar merger of Aetna and US Health Care.
- Developed creative methods to overcome workplace negativity and help staff focus on work objectives.

Military:

- Enlisted in the U.S. Army Reserves, 399th Combat Support Hospital, and served for six years.
- Provided medical support for Operation Just Cause, (the U.S. invasion of Panama to remove General Manuel Noriega), in December

1989 with the 399th Combat Support Hospital, U.S. Army.

- Earned an Army Commendation medal during Operation Starburst, Fort Hood Texas, July1988.
- Created and delivered to numerous Army reserve units an innovative soldier training method for military preparedness in a game show format called the "BuzzBowl."

Sales:

- Worked for five years as a physician recruiter in the managed care industry.
- Conducted presentations to physicians and hospital administrators to encourage network participation.
- Awarded the 1996 Recruiter of the Year Award at Aetna after achieving 105% territory network growth.

Clinical Health Care:

- Earned a degree in radiologic technology and is a licensed radiographer R.T.(R).
- Delivered hands-on care for patients in both military and civilian

clinical healthcare settings.

- Served as a staff radiology technologist for a 500-bed acute care facility.
- Operated mobile MRI units and performed exams for a network of over ten hospitals.

Kevin Stacey lives with his wife, Laura, and three children, Olivia, Zachary, and Colin in New England.

About TrainRight, Inc.

TrainRight, Inc. is a professional education and consulting providing customized training programs, coaching initiatives, keynote presentations and group seminars. We specialize in eliminating self-created problems and distractions that impede productivity and developing the cognitive skills of focus, concentration, creative problem solving, and critical and positive thinking. We assist our clients with individual effectiveness, conflict resolution, time management, stress management, team building, professional and effective workplace communications, leadership development, coaching and feedback.

We deliver on-site time management training, stress management training, and consulting to your organization to help you and your staff:

- Work at full capacity and get results.

- Eliminate costly distractions and get focused on the goals of the organization.

- Stop wasting valuable time feeling overwhelmed or bothered.

- Reduce workplace negativity and improve morale.

For more information, visit www.trainrightinc.com or call 1-800-603-7168, FAX 617-687-1295, or email: info@trainrightinc.com

Program highlights:

These program highlights are for the most popular programs we do. We are also very happy to customize and tailor a program to your specific needs and challenges. We will go to great lengths to achieve the goals of your training session or meeting. Any program can be delivered in any format that would be unproblematic for your workflow- whether it's a keynote, full day, half-day, multiple days, or a full day with half the staff in the morning and half in the afternoon,

Time Management Training

Boost your effectiveness, efficiency and self-discipline. Identify the most important tasks and key time wasters. Discover new ways to allocate and manage your time, deal with challenging deadlines, imposing workloads, interruptions and ridiculous meetings. Handle even the most difficult projects and workloads with a manageable, one-step-at-a-time plan. Stick with the plan and focus on it with discipline. Set clear boundaries with others to not allow interruptions or other distractions to diminish your focus. Move from feeling overwhelmed and spinning your wheels to taking action.

Executive Coaching

- This is an interactive process that helps individuals develop more rapidly and produce more satisfying results.

- The primary initial objective in most coaching situations is the development of self-awareness.

- This involves taking an honest look at the way in which personal characteristics and behaviors impact on decision-making, relating to others, planning, and all other executive functions.

- Another common objective for many executives is recognizing and overcoming self-limiting and self-defeating behaviors.

- Identify the situations and people that drain your energy along with new strategies to more effectively deal with them

- Coaching is a unique opportunity to be reminded what we can do, that's under our control, to make things better for ourselves along with what we can stop doing that accomplishes nothing.

Stress Management Training

Increase your staff's mental toughness and decrease the likelihood they will be distracted by negative emotions while under pressure. Have the members of your workforce spend more time being focused and productive and less time feeling annoyed or frustrated. Learn to stop "dramatizing the deadlines" and feeling overwhelmed. Set clear, measurable and specific goals, establish priorities, focus on one task at a time, and overcome procrastination.

How to Stay Motivated and Energized in Challenging Times

Practical techniques to boost your life's satisfaction, serenity, and success. Cope more easily with overwhelming workloads, unrealistic expectations, and the daily dramas that cause stress and burnout. Learn what you can do that's under your control to make things better, and what you can stop doing that makes things worse.

Dealing with Difficult People/ Conflict Resolution Skills

Essential training for today's collaborative, team-oriented workplace. Conflict can have a devastating effect on productivity, morale, teamwork and ultimately your organization's bottom line. But when handled the right way, conflict can actually energize, produce change, and even bring together opposing parties.

Overcome Workplace Negativity

Real-world, practical advice on dealing with negativity when it creeps into your team, department, or organization, to include: how to spot and fix negative attitudes before they fester and become contagious, methods to help you hold people accountable for their negative behaviors, and ways to transform negativity into optimism.

Assertive Communication Skills: Critical Discussions

Life gets easier and you live with less resentment when you can speak up for yourself in an assertive and professional way – both at work and at home. If you ever felt as though you wished there was a "pause" and "rewind" button in life so you could go back and say what you really wished you said to someone, then this topic is for you.

From Management to Leadership

Management: to direct or control an action. Leadership: to bring a person to a place. Get the essential skills and perspective to lead your employees to a place of believing in the company, your leadership, and wanting not only to do the work, but wanting to work there.

Speed Reading

In today's fast paced, information-driven environment, we have less time than ever for keeping up-to-date. Emails, policies, trade publications, newspapers, journals, and other business materials pile up in our in-boxes. It's becomes a real problem, especially when everything changes so quickly. This course is the solution, as it's designed to enable you to be able to read faster and retain more. Participants learn the tools and techniques to double and even triple their current reading speed. The course begins by measuring your current rate and helps you learn to improve your reading speed while increasing how much information you retain at the same time. No gimmicks, no machines. Simple methods that can work for you and your staff. Most college-educated adults read between 225 and 350 words per minute, but speed readers can read more than 1,000 words per minute with higher comprehension.

Team Building

In today's lean and competitive environment, it's critical that employees feel part of a cohesive team that is working together for common goals. This training session gets employees out of their usual routines and has the minter act with each other to build bonds and relationships that withstand pressure. It also boosts retention, teamwork, and contributes to a positive and fun working environment.

Buzz Bowl Team Building Game Show

Looking for an innovative, fun idea to spruce up your next training or corporate event? The Buzz Bowl is a parody of Jeopardy® with up to four teams of up to six members each, each with their own electrical buzzer. It's a highly effective training technique that boosts retention, teamwork, and contributes to a positive and fun working environment. We have been doing this for fifteen years in settings as diverse as the U.S. Army and corporate America, and it has always been a hit!

Boost Self- Esteem; Decrease Personal Insecurity and Anxiety, Increase Productivity

Find the inspiration to treat yourself better and find your own happiness within, therefore becoming more effective in your external interactions. The more secure and centered in yourself you are, the more capable you become and the more energy you free up to be productive.

Advanced Business Writing

This business writing seminar is not another day at school. These sessions are highly interactive, include group activities, and provide practical tactics that will immediately improve a participant's writing. Business writing training covers emails, letters, proposals, and reports. We start at the beginning with the writer's perspective, address audience needs, and then proceed to the specific "must-have" skills required by clear and concise business writers. Also included are grammar tidbits to review, common errors in spelling, grammar rules, and word usage. The seminar rounds out the skills base with a proofreading section designed to produce a more polished and professional document.

Change Management

Change is an inevitable part of life and realistically we only have two choices when it comes to dealing with change: fight it and let fear keep us stuck in the status quo, or embrace it and view it as not only exciting, but what makes life worth living.

Self-discipline and Emotional Control

Learn methods for reducing compulsive behavior and techniques to remain in control and ease pressure. This workshop is a powerful system based on rational-emotive behavior therapy and will help change your negative behaviors permanently.

Powerful Presentation Skills

Whether the goal is to make sales, develop rapport with customers, or persuade an audience, the ability to present your ideas in a confident manner is essential to career success. This workshop is designed to help you communicate with more composure, confidence, and in a more compelling manner. It will help you unearth self-defeating attitudes and replace them with positive expectations. You'll also get tips to help you deal with trembling hands, butterflies, and other nervous symptoms.

Customer Service

The program helps to build a solid foundation of skills and techniques which impact the customer's perception of your organization. Learn to handle difficult customers, make every customer (internal and/or external) interaction a productive experience, and offer a positive alternative to every customer request. Avoid passing the stress of one situation on to the next, use personality to create a "business friendly" environment, eliminate technical jargon and frustration and learn to value people over paperwork.

Mental Toughness in the Workplace

Studies show that 77% of what we think about is negative or counterproductive. Negative thinking is a tremendous cost to both individuals and organizations since all success or failure is based on mental principals. We have all heard of the solution—to maintain a "positive mental attitude." But what does that really mean? How do we do that in a practical sense? This workshop or keynote presentation offers a step-by-step process for tapping into the power of our minds to program ourselves for success and peak performance.

Emotional Intelligence

Emotional intelligence is a set of competencies that enhance your ability to relate positively to others in the workplace. People with high emotional intelligence are adept at using empathy and constructive communication to create a collaborative, cooperative work environment. They naturally relate well to others; are able to accomplish more through encouragement and persuasion; and excel at inspiring, guiding, and leading others to achieve their best work. As performers, they tend to be flexible, adaptive, self-motivated, and confident.

Managing Virtual and Remote Workers

You cannot manage employees who work remotely the same way you manage those you see in the workplace every day. Email, phone and video communication pale in effectiveness compared with live human interaction. How do you know employees are working diligently when you cannot see them? Managing a team that is either completely or partially off-site has its challenges, and it is your job to rise to those challenges. This seminar is packed with all the how-to techniques, tips, and tricks you need to keep your off-site employees energized, productive, and fully integrated into the team. The human side of management has always been and will always be the most important part of a manager's job. It is not easy when employees work remotely — but it can be done. This training is the best and easiest way to become a master at managing a virtual team.

Fundamentals of Project Management

This course is a practical, hands-on, case study based approach to managing projects that focuses on the principles of project management. It provides practical examples of project planning concepts of scope, budget, schedule development, risk, quality, and change control. The course provides an overview of key project concepts and terminology which helps individuals effectively initiate, plan, execute, monitor, control, and close a project. This hands-on class provides the knowledge, insights, and techniques needed in today's project driven environment. The largest gains in project success come with a focus on the fundamentals—the process, the vocabulary, the tools and techniques of achievement.

Critical Thinking and Problem Solving

Critical thinking is the mental process of discovery, analysis, and evaluation. It involves reflective judgment that considers evidence, context, completeness, and relevance of information, biases, and emotional issues. This course provides practical and effective ways to think and problem solve using critical thinking skills.

Coaching and Counseling Skills for Supervisors and Managers

This workshop will help you to develop coaching and counseling skills that improve employee and workplace performance. Be more effective and confident in coaching, counseling, criticizing, training and the career development of your employees.

Discipline and Attitude Problems in the Workplace for Supervisors and Managers

This human resource seminar focuses on solving the problem behavior rather than "punishment" (which is a waste of time and money). This workshop centers on respect, responsibility and creating a context where the employee who is causing a problem agrees to be the one who solves it. Supervisors will learn how to prepare for disciplinary meetings, how to conduct them, and what to do when they are over.

www.trainrightinc.com

87303000R00088

Made in the USA
Columbia, SC
23 January 2018